Picnics and Barbecues

Savory meals at home and away
Recipe Cards by Herbert H. Wise & Cecile Lamalle
With Recipes by Emilie Tolley

quick fox

New York London

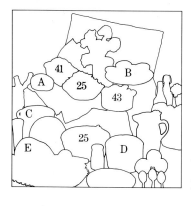

A. **Swiss Potato Loaf see**
   Winter Soups and Breads
B. **Chocolate Mousse see**
   Sweet Touches
C. **Leek and Potatoe Soup see**
   Winter Soups and Breads
D. **Tomatoes Vinaigrette see**
   Vegetable Delights
E. **Rye Bread see *Winter Soups**
   *and Breads***

Some of the photographs and recipes in this series are from *Kitchen Detail*, by the same authors. *Kitchen Detail*, which features kitchen design, equipment and food preparation, is available in bookstores and wherever fine design books are sold.

In these countries available through:
Gage Trade Publishing, P.O. Box 5000
164 Commander Blvd, Agincourt, Ontario MIS 3C7, Canada
Book Sales, Ltd., 78 Newman Street, London WIP 3LA, England

Designed by Joseph L. Santoro
Styling by Jamie Simpson
Photography by Herbert H. Wise

Printed in Japan

Barbecue Tips

Barbecue. Whether it was inspired by the French words *barbe à queue* (head to tail) or *barbacoa*, the wodden framework the Spanish used to roast meats over an open fire, it's now an All-American pastime. It is also a truly international way of cooking. In almost every country in the world the streets are filled with the wonderful aromas of local fresh foods being grilled with the seasonings of the country: sardines in Portugal, duck and pork in China, lamb in Morroco, fish in France. The variety is endless because almost any fresh food can be prepared over a grill. With a good fire and the right equipment, it's an easy way to prepare a delicious meal. Here are some tips to help make you an expert on the grill.

Before you start cooking, grease the grill. It will prevent the food from sticking and facilitate cleaning up.

Good charcoal briquets are the best fuel. Pile them into a pyramid to start the fire. When they're ignited, spread them into a circle just slightly larger than the food to be cooked.

Don't rush your fire. Light the coals about 40 minutes before you want to start cooking. The coals should be glowing red inside with a covering of gray ash. Do not begin grilling while the coals are flaming or still have black areas that are not ignited.

If you're cooking something that takes a long time, you can keep the fire going evenly by adding coals around the outer edges and moving them in under the food as they're ready. If you want to cool the fire down, space the coals farther apart. Tap the coals periodically to shake off the ashes that can smother the fire.

Generally, place the grill about 6 inches above the coals. If you want to cook slower or faster, you can adjust the height of the grill. You can also judge the heat of the fire by holding your hand, palm down, about 6 inches above the fire. If you can leave it there 2 to 3 seconds, the fire is just about right.

Besides the grill itself, you don't need much equipment to be an accomplished barbecue chef. Most important is a pair of tongs. They are much better than a fork for turning foods. Unlike a fork, they won't pierce the meat, allowing juices to escape, and they help keep foil packets of tender fish and vegetables intact. A hinged grill is also handy to have for grilling some vegetables and fish. Always keep a spray bottle of water at hand to keep flames under control, but avoid soaking the coals.

One last hint: To give extra flavor to foods, toss fresh or dried herbs on the fire while grilling. Their flavor and aroma will enhance the foods during cooking. You also can make a brush from sprigs of rosemary or thyme and use it to apply marinade during cooking, then toss it into the fire for one last burst of flavor.

Minted Lamb Chops

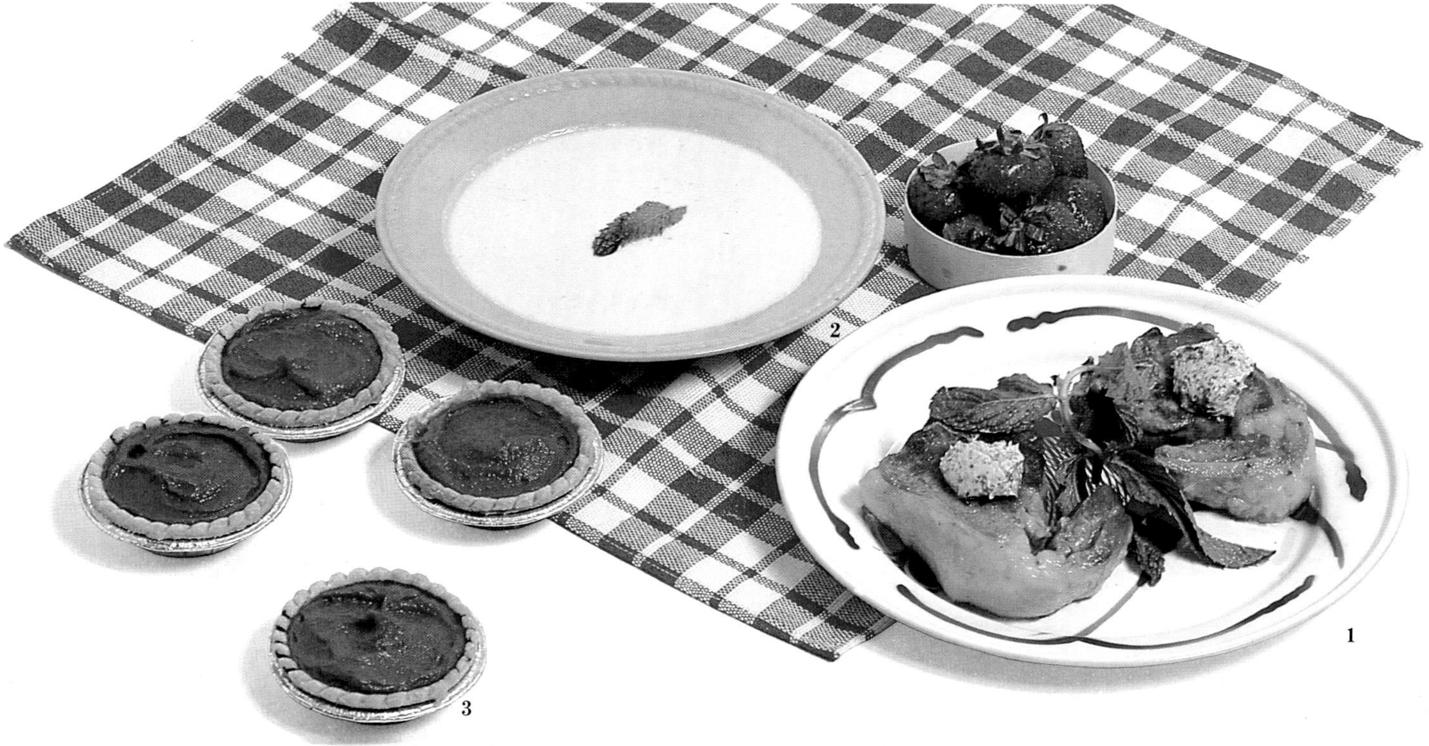

Mint & Lamb Chops

1. Minted Lamb Chops

½ cup mint, chopped
1 clove garlic, minced
3 Tablespoons lemon juice
¾ cup olive oil
Salt and freshly ground pepper to taste
6 loin lamb chops, 1½-inches thick

Minted Butter

1 stick butter, softened
2 Tablespoons fresh mint, chopped
1 Tablespoon parsley, chopped
1 small clove garlic, minced

Method

1. Combine mint, garlic, lemon juice and oil in food processor or blender. Add salt and pepper to taste. Pour over the lamb chops and marinate at room temperature 2 to 3 hours.
2. While chops marinate, prepare Minted Butter by blending herbs and butter in a food processor. Chill until ready to use.
3. When ready to grill, blot chops dry on paper towels. Grill over hot coals, turning twice, about 8 minutes on each side. Test for doneness. Serve with a bit of Minted Butter on each.

6 servings

2. Cucumber Soup

3 cucumbers
5 cups chicken broth
¼ pound potatoes
1½ cups strawberries
¼ cup sour cream
Salt and freshly ground pepper to taste
Garnish: Chopped fresh mint

Method

1. Peel, dice and seed cucumbers. Cook in 1 cup broth about 10 minutes, or until tender.
2. Peel potatoes and cook in boiling water until done. Drain. Combine in food processor or blender potatoes, cucumbers, their broth, and 2 additional cups of broth. Empty into bowl.
3. Put strawberries and remaining 2 cups of broth in processor and purée. Add to cucumber-potato mixture and put through a sieve. Stir in sour cream and taste for seasoning.
4. Chill at least 3 hours. Serve garnished with fresh mint.

6 to 8 servings

3. Tomato and Basil Tartlets

2 Tablespoons olive oil
1 small onion, chopped
1 clove garlic, crushed
1 red pepper, diced
1½ pounds tomatoes, peeled, seeded and chopped
4 sprigs fresh basil, chopped
1 teaspoon sugar
1 bay leaf
1 teaspoon lemon juice
1 Tablespoon tomato paste
6 baked tartlet shells

Method

1. Cook the onions and garlic in hot oil until soft but not brown. Add the diced pepper and cook another 3 minutes. Add tomatoes, basil, sugar, bay leaf, lemon juice and tomato paste. Cook slowly 1 hour, stirring occasionally, or until almost all the moisture has evaporated and mixture is reduced to a paste. Remove bay leaf.
2. Fill the shells with sauce and decorate each one with a bay leaf.

6 servings

Gingered Ham Steaks

1. Gingered Ham Steaks

1½ cups unsweetened pineapple juice
½ cup cider vinegar
¼ cup vegetable oil
⅓ cup honey
¾ cup gingersnap crumbs
2 cooked ham slices, 1-inch thick

Method
1. Mix the pineapple juice, vinegar, oil and honey and simmer 2 to 3 minutes. Stir in gingersnap crumbs.
2. Paint the ham slices with mixture and broil over medium coals 10 minutes on each side, basting with remaining sauce.

6 to 8 servings

2. Grilled Corn with Herbs

6 ears of corn
6 Tablespoons butter
2 Tablespoons chives, chopped
2 Tablespoons parsley, chopped
Salt and freshly ground pepper to taste

Method
1. Clean husks and silk from corn.
2. Blend butter with herbs and seasonings. Spread a tablespoonful on each ear and wrap individually in heavy-duty aluminum foil.
3. Grill 15 to 20 minutes, turning occasionally.

6 servings

3. Baked Peaches

1 stick butter
1 cup light brown sugar
6 peaches, peeled and sliced
½ teaspoon cinnamon
4 Tablespoons cognac

Method
1. Cream butter and sugar. Put each sliced peach in a square of heavy-duty aluminum foil. Divide butter and sugar mixture among the six peaches. Sprinkle each with cinnamon and seal the packets.
2. Cook over a low fire 12 to 15 minutes, or until peaches are cooked and butter and sugar are melted. Remove from fire.
3. Heat cognac over fire. Pour some into each packet and flame.

6 servings

Grilled Lamb Chops

1. Grilled Lamb Chops with Mustard Butter

¼ pound butter
⅓ cup mustard
1 clove garlic

½ medium onion
6 loin lamb chops, 1½ inches thick
Garnish: watercress

Method

1. Combine butter, mustard, garlic and onion in a food processor or blender to make Mustard Butter.
2. Spread over both sides of lamb chops and let stand for 1 hour.
3. Grill over hot coals, turning twice, about 8 minutes on each side. Test for doneness. Serve with extra Mustard Butter on the side.

6 servings

2. Cherry Tomatoes Provençal

1½ pints cherry tomatoes
6 Tablespoons olive oil
⅓ cup onion, finely minced
1 large clove garlic, finely minced

⅓ cup parsley, chopped
1 teaspoon fresh thyme, chopped
¾ cup soft bread crumbs
Salt and freshly ground pepper to taste

Method

1. Arrange cherry tomatoes in a single layer on six 12x12-inch lightly oiled squares of heavy-duty aluminum foil.
2. Mix remaining ingredients and sprinkle over tomatoes.
3. Seal packets and cook over medium coals 8 to 10 minutes.

6 servings

3. Chocolate Chip Pie

4 Tablespoons butter
1 cup sugar
3 eggs, beaten
¾ cup light corn syrup
1 teaspoon vanilla

¼ teaspoon salt
½ cup chocolate chips
½ cup pecans, chopped
2 Tablespoons Puerto Rican rum
1 unbaked pie shell (10-inches)

Method

1. Cream butter. Gradually beat in sugar. Add beaten eggs, corn syrup, vanilla and salt. Mix well, then stir in chocolate chips, pecans and rum.
2. Pour filling into shell and bake in 375° oven 40 to 45 minutes.

9

Soused Shrimp

1. Soused Shrimp

3 pounds medium shrimp, cooked and shelled
3 medium onions, thinly sliced
4 slices of lemon
½ cup parsley, chopped

Salt and freshly ground pepper to taste
¼ teaspoon Tabasco sauce
Olive oil
3 bay leaves

Method

Layer the shrimp, onion, lemon and parsley in a serving bowl. Add salt and pepper, Tabasco sauce and enough olive oil to cover. Top with bay leaves and marinate 6 to 8 hours. Serve with lots of good, dark bread.

6 to 8 servings

2. Dilly Pea Salad

1 cup fresh peas, or 1 package (10 ounces) small frozen peas
½ cup fresh sugar snap peas, or snow peas
¼ cup sour cream
2 Tablespoons fresh dill, chopped

2 Tablespoons fresh chives, chopped
½ teaspoon curry powder
Salt and freshly ground pepper to taste
Boston lettuce
Garnish: chopped dill

Method

1. If using frozen peas, defrost them. If using fresh peas, blanch them 2 to 3 minutes, then cool.
2. Combine the sour cream, dill, chives, curry powder and salt and pepper. Mix well. Blend with the peas and snap peas, tossing carefully to avoid mashing the peas. Refrigerate 10 to 15 minutes or until ready to use.
3. To serve, line a bowl with lettuce and fill with peas mixture. Garnish with dill.

6 servings

3. Pecan Bars

1 cup all-purpose flour
¼ teaspoon baking powder
½ cup butter, softened
⅓ cup brown sugar
½ cup pecans, finely chopped

Topping

2 eggs
¾ cup brown sugar
3 Tablespoons flour
½ teaspoon salt
1 teaspoon vanilla
1 cup pecans, coarsely chopped

Method

1. Combine all the ingredients for bars and work them together until crumbly. Press the mixture into the bottom of a lightly greased 7½x11½x2-inch pan and bake in a preheated 350° oven 10 minutes.
2. Prepare topping while bar mixture is baking. Beat the eggs well and stir in the corn syrup, brown sugar, flour, salt and vanilla. Top the bar mixture and sprinkle with pecans. Bake another 25 minutes. Cool and cut into bars.

16 bars

Veal Roll

1. Veal Roll

2 pounds thin veal cutlets
¼ pound salami
¼ pound prosciutto or cooked ham
¼ cup bread crumbs
2 cloves garlic, minced
4 Tablespoons parsley, chopped
2 Tablespoons basil, chopped
5 hard-cooked eggs

Salt and freshly ground pepper to taste
4 slices bacon
2 cups chunked fresh tomatoes with juice or canned stewed tomatoes (containing 2 whole cloves garlic and 2 basil leaves)
Garnish: parsley or watercress

Method

1. Overlap cutlets lengthwise on a piece of waxed paper. Pound cutlets and overlapping edges well.

2. Layer salami on top of veal, and ham on top of salami. Combine crumbs, garlic, parsley and basil and sprinkle over ham. Arrange eggs in a row down the center. Roll up very carefully as for a jellyroll, using the paper to help roll. Make sure the eggs remain in the center. Tie the meat in several places to keep the roll in shape.

3. Place in baking dish and cover top with bacon and tomato sauce. Bake in 350° oven 1 hour. Remove from pan and cool overnight.

4. Slice and serve garnished with parsley or watercress.

6 to 8 servings

2. Dilled Potato and Egg Salad

2½ pounds small new potatoes, quartered
6 hard-cooked eggs, quartered
1 cup ripe French olives
1 red onion, thinly sliced

5 Tablespoons fresh dill, chopped
1½ cups yogurt
6 Tablespoons olive oil
1 teaspoon salt
Freshly ground pepper to taste

Method

1. Scrub potatoes and peel a thin strip around the center of each. Boil until tender and drain.

2. Place potatoes, eggs, olives and onion in a serving bowl. Sprinkle with 1 Tablespoon dill.

3. Blend the yogurt, olive oil, salt and pepper with remaining dill. Put in a small bowl and serve with the salad.

6 servings

3. Chocolate Mousse

8 eggs, separated
½ pound unsweetened chocolate

1 cup heavy cream
1 cup confectioners' sugar

Method

1. Melt chocolate in a double boiler.

2. Place in the container of a blender the egg yolks, chocolate, cream and sugar and blend at lowest speed for a few minutes. Add unbeaten whites and blend 1 or 2 minutes longer.

3. Pour into individual containers and chill overnight. Serve this rich mixture in small quantities.

6 to 8 servings

13

Teriyaki Burgers

1. Teriyaki Burgers

3 pounds ground beef
1 cup soy sauce
½ cup sherry

2 teaspoons ground ginger
4 cloves garlic, pressed
Oil
Garnish: cherry tomatoes, watercress

Method

1. Mix together all ingredients, except beef, to make Teriyaki sauce.

2. Combine the ground beef with ½ cup sauce. Mix well and shape into patties. Brush patties with oil. Broil burgers to desired degree of doneness, brushing every two minutes with oil. Serve with remaining Teriyaki sauce, and garnished with cherry tomatoes and watercress.

6 to 8 servings

2. Broccoli with Sesame Sauce

2 pounds broccoli
4 Tablespoons soy sauce

2 Tablespoons sesame oil
½ cup sesame seeds, toasted
1 teaspoon honey

Method

1. Trim and discard tough broccoli stems. Cut broccoli into bite-size pieces. Steam 4 to 5 minutes or until tender but not soft. Chill.

2. Mix remaining ingredients and pour over chilled broccoli. Marinate at least 1 hour before serving.

6 servings

3. Baked Bananas

6 Tablespoons butter
6 Tablespoons sugar
6 bananas, peeled and cut in half lengthwise

½ teaspoon cinnamon
½ cup Barbados rum
6 lime wedges

Method

1. Cream butter and sugar. Place each banana in a square of heavy-duty aluminum foil. Spread some butter and sugar on each. Sprinkle with cinnamon. Seal the packets.

2. Cook over low fire 10 to 12 minutes, or until the bananas are cooked.

3. Meanwhile heat rum over fire. Remove packets from fire, open and pour a little hot rum in each and flame. Serve with lime wedges.

6 servings

Clams and Oysters Casino & Swordfish Steaks Veronique

1. Clams and Oysters Casino

24 soft or hard-shell clams
24 oysters

Casino Butter

1 pound salted butter, softened
½ green Bell pepper, diced
½ red pimento, diced
2 shallots, finely chopped
2 Tablespoons parsley, chopped
4 Tablespoons lemon juice
2 Tablespoons Worcestershire sauce

Method

1. Scrub the clams and oysters well.
2. Prepare the Casino Butter by mixing together all the ingredients. Roll into a cylinder the breadth of a silver dollar. Wrap and store in freezer until ready to use.
3. Steam the mollusks open. Discard the top shells and lay mollusks in a flat pan. Cover each with a slice of the butter mixture and set the pan on the grill until the butter melts.

8 servings

Note: Casino Butter is excellent for steaks, chops, fish, chicken and vegetables.

2. Swordfish Steaks Veronique

8 swordfish steaks
Oil for basting

Garnish : 8 small clusters green seedless grapes; 8 small bunches curly parsley; 4 lemons (halved)

Method

1. Brush the swordfish liberally with oil. Grill over hot coals about 5 minutes on each side and baste frequently.
2. To serve, garnish each steak with grapes, parsley and lemon.

8 servings

3. North African Salad

3 tomatoes
2 green Bell peppers
1 sweet onion
1 large cucumber, peeled

North African Dressing

Grated peel of 2 lemons
¼ cup lemon juice
1½ teaspoon salt
⅛ teaspoon red pepper or Tabasco sauce
2 cloves garlic, minced
¾ cup olive oil
½ teaspoon ground coriander
½ teaspoon ground cumin
½ teaspoon dried mustard
1 teaspoon sugar
½ teaspoon paprika

Method

Mix together ingredients for dressing. Slice or cube the vegetables and place in a serving bowl. Serve with dressing.

4 servings

4. Double Corn Biscuits

1⅛ cups all-purpose flour
1 cup yellow corn meal
3 Tablespoons sugar
3 teaspoons baking powder
½ teaspoon salt
1 egg
1 cup milk
3 Tablespoons melted butter, cooled
1 cup cream-style corn
1 teaspoon fresh thyme, chopped

Method

1. Sift together flour, corn meal, sugar, baking powder and salt.
2. Beat the egg and milk in bowl. Stir in the butter and mix in the corn and thyme. Add the dry ingredients and beat into batter.
3. Drop by the tablespoonful on a greased baking sheet. Bake in a preheated 400° oven about 15 minutes, or until tops are brown.

24 biscuits

Meat Brochettes

1. Skewers of Beef, Peppers and Tomato

Alternate cubes of meat or ground beef balls on skewers with pepper and tomato slices. Brush with oil while grilling.

2. Ham Chunks with Peppers

Skewer chunks of ham, red and green Bell peppers (4 chunks ham per person). Brush with sauce mixed with ½ cup oil, ½ cup soy sauce and 2 Tablespoons Dijon-style mustard.

3. Pineapple and Chicken

Plan on ½ chicken breast per person. Cube skinned chicken and alternate on skewer with pineapple chunks. Brush with a mixture of ½ cup oil and ½ cup soy sauce while cooking. Chicken may be marinated in this mixture for several hours before grilling.

4. Chilly Yogurt Soup

3 Tablespoons butter
9 green onions, chopped
1¼ cup spinach, chopped*
¼ cup sorrel, chopped*
4 cucumbers, peeled and chopped

3 large potatoes, peeled and quartered
4½ cups chicken broth
1½ cups yogurt
Salt and freshly ground pepper to taste
Garnish: watercress

Method

1. Sauté the green onions in butter until soft but not brown. Add spinach, sorrel, cucumbers and potatoes. Add the chicken broth and bring to a boil. Lower heat and simmer, covered, until potatoes are tender. Cool slightly.

2. Purée potatoes in a food processor or blender. Add yogurt and mix well. Chill for several hours before serving. Garnish with watercress.

6 servings

*If sorrel is not available, use all spinach and add 2 Tablespoons lemon juice with the yogurt.

5. Picnic Cake

½ cup butter
1½ cups light brown sugar
2 eggs
2½ cups flour
1 Tablespoon baking powder
½ teaspoon salt

1 teaspoon vanilla extract
1 cup milk
10 large marshmallows, cut in half
½ cup dark brown sugar
½ cup pecans or walnuts, coarsely chopped

Method

1. Cream butter and sugar until light and fluffy. Add eggs one at a time, beating well after each addition. Sift flour, baking powder, and salt. Mix vanilla into milk. Add dry ingredients and milk mixture alternately to butter and sugar, beating smooth after each addition.

2. Pour batter into greased and floured 9x9-inch pan. To top batter, place marshmallows with round side up. Mix sugar with nuts and sprinkle on top. Bake in 350° oven 50 minutes.

Grilled Brochettes

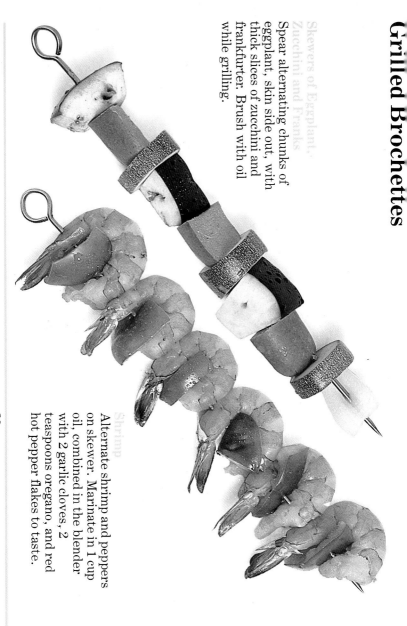

Skewers of Eggplant, Zucchini and Franks
Spear alternating chunks of eggplant, skin side out, with thick slices of zucchini and frankfurter. Brush with oil while grilling.

Shrimp
Alternate shrimp and peppers on skewer. Marinate in 1 cup oil, combined in the blender with 2 garlic cloves, 2 teaspoons oregano, and red hot pepper flakes to taste.

Grilled Brochettes

Mushrooms and Bacon
Cut off mushroom stems, wrap each mushroom in bacon, skewer and grill.

Scallops
Alternate scallops on skewers with reconstituted seaweed and cherry tomatoes. Brush with Teriyaki sauce while grilling.

21

Indian Kebabs

1. Indian Kebabs

2 pounds lean ground beef
2 teaspoons coriander leaves, chopped
1 large onion, finely grated,
2 cloves garlic, mashed
½ teaspoon powdered ginger
½ teaspoon tumeric

½ teaspoon ground coriander
½ teaspoon dried red pepper flakes
Salt to taste
4 Tablespoons yogurt
2 large green Bell peppers, cleaned and cut into wedges
2 large tomatoes, cut into wedges

Method

1. Mix all the ingredients in a bowl, using yogurt as a binder.
2. Form the mixture into small sausages and press around skewers to form balls. Alternate balls with pepper and tomato chunks.
3. Grill over coals, turning once, until well browned and done (about 5 minutes).

6 servings

2. Lentil Salad

3 cups quick cooking lentils
1 onion stuck with 4 cloves
2 cloves garlic, sliced
2 bay leaves
3 Tablespoons cider vinegar
½ cup olive oil

Salt and freshly ground pepper to taste
3 Tablespoons parsley, chopped
½ cup Roquefort cheese, crumbled
6 radishes, thinly sliced
½ cucumber, thinly sliced
2 medium red onions, thinly sliced

Method

1. Put lentils in a pot with enough water to cover. Add onion, garlic and bay leaves and salt to taste. Cook about 25 minutes until tender but not mushy. Drain. Remove onion, garlic and bay leaves. Cool and chill lentils.
2. Check seasoning and add salt and pepper to taste.
3. Add the remaining ingredients and toss gently. Marinate several hours or overnight.

6 to 8 servings

3. Pineapple Rum Cup

½ cup sugar
½ cup water
½ cup Puerto Rican rum

1 pineapple, cubed
3 bananas, diced
Lemon sherbert or vanilla ice cream (optional)

Method

1. Boil the sugar and water together about 5 minutes. Cool and stir in rum.
2. Place the fruit in a bowl and pour the rum syrup over the fruit. Marinate 3 to 4 hours.
3. Serve plain, or with sherbert or ice cream.

6 servings

Oriental Soy Chicken Chunks

1. Oriental Soy Chicken Chunks

16 chicken thighs
2 medium onions, thinly sliced
6 to 8 generous slices fresh ginger
½ cup white wine
¼ cup soy sauce
Garnish: 1 green Bell pepper, sliced (optional)

Batter
1 cup flour
4 eggs
6 Tablespoons chicken broth
Peanut oil

Method

1. Place chicken in baking pan. Cover with onions, ginger, wine, soy sauce, and pepper. Cover and bake in 350° oven until tender (about 1 hour).

2. Reserve cooking broth. Skin thighs and remove center bones.

3. Prepare batter of flour, eggs and broth. Dip chicken chunks in batter. Deep fry in oil until brown and drain on paper towels. Serve garnished with green pepper.

6 to 8 servings

2. Green Bean Salad

1½ pounds very young, fresh green beans, topped and tailed
⅓ cup fruity olive oil
2 Tablespoons herb vinegar
3 shallots, finely minced
Salt and freshly ground pepper to taste
¼ cup chopped parsley

Method

Bring several quarts of water to a boil and add the green beans. Cook them a very short time — test after 3 minutes — in rapidly boiling water. Drain while still crunchy, and plunge in ice water to stop the cooking. Drain again, and dress, while still somewhat warm, with the olive oil, vinegar, shallots, parsley, salt and pepper.

4 servings

3. Pineapple Squares

2 cups butter
4 cups all-purpose flour
1 cup sour cream
1 teaspoon vanilla
1 cup sugar
3 Tablespoons cornstarch
42 ounces canned crushed pineapple, well drained

Method

1. Mix butter and flour to a coarse cornmeal consistency. Add sour cream and vanilla and mix well. It may be necessary to mix the stiff dough with your hands to get it well blended. Refrigerate dough for 2 hours.

2. Combine sugar and cornstarch in a saucepan. Add pineapple and cook, stirring constantly, until thickened and clear. Cool.

3. Roll half of the dough into a 15½x10½-inch rectangle on waxed paper. Place in a shallow pan the same size. Spread pineapple over dough. Roll remaining dough to same size and place on top of pineapple.

4. Bake in 325° oven 25 minutes or until golden. Sprinkle with powdered sugar and cut to squares.

About 4½ dozen

3

Trout Wrapped in Bacon and Ham

1. Trout Wrapped in Bacon and Ham

8 fresh trout, cleaned	8 slices quality smoked ham
Salt and freshly ground pepper to taste	8 slices bacon

Method

1. Sprinkle trout cavities with salt and pepper. Wrap each fish with a slice of ham and a slice of bacon.
2. Place trout on a folding grill and cook for approximately 5 to 7 minutes on each side. When done, flesh should flake easily with a fork.

8 servings

2. Herbed Steamed Vegetables

½ bunch broccoli	
½ head cauliflower	
2 large carrots, quartered	
2 handfuls sugar snap peas	
2 handfuls green beans	
1 handful thin asparagus	
1 yellow squash, thinly sliced	
1 zucchini, thinly sliced	

Herbed Oil

1 Tablespoon fresh thyme
1½ Tablespoons fresh marjoram
1½ Tablespoons fresh sage
1½ Tablespoons fresh savory
1 Tablespoon salt
2 teaspoons freshly ground black pepper
½ cup olive oil

Method

1. Steam the broccoli, cauliflower and carrots 12 to 15 minutes.
2. Steam the peas, beans and asparagus about 10 minutes.
3. Steam the squash and zucchini about 5 minutes.
4. Rinse vegetables under cold water immediately after steaming to retard cooking. Drain and arrange on a large platter.
5. For Herbed Oil, grind all herbs and salt and pepper to a paste with the olive oil in a food processor or blender.
6. Dribble the Herbed Oil over vegetables just before serving, or set oil in separate cruet and let guests help themselves.

3. Lemon Bread

6 Tablespoons unsalted butter	1½ cups all-purpose flour
1 cup sugar	1 teaspoon baking powder
2 eggs	Pinch of salt
½ cup milk	1 Tablespoon lemon peel, finely grated

Method

1. Cream butter and sugar. Beat in eggs, one at a time. Add milk, blending well. Mix in dry ingredients. Add lemon peel.
2. Pour into a greased and floured 9x5-inch loaf pan. Bake in a 350° oven 1 hour.
3. To mix topping blend sugar with lemon juice into a thin paste.
4. When bread is done, cool slightly and remove from pan.

Veal Chops with Rosemary

1. Veal Chops with Rosemary

6 veal chops, 1-inch thick*

Marinade

⅓ cup olive oil
4 Tablespoons tomato paste
2 Tablespoons lemon juice
3 Tablespoons fresh rosemary, chopped (or 1 Tablespoon powdered)
2 Tablespoons red wine vinegar
Salt and freshly ground pepper to taste
Garnish: cucumber slices

Rosemary Butter

6 Tablespoons sweet butter
1 Tablespoon rosemary, chopped
2 Tablespoon parsely, chopped

Method

1. Combine ingredients for marinade. Pour over chops and refrigerate overnight.
2. Blend ingredients for Rosemary Butter and chill.
3. Cook chops over medium coals, about 8 minutes on each side, while basting with marinade. Serve with Rosemary Butter.

6 servings

*If you prefer to use lamb riblets instead of veal chops, substitute 4 pounds lamb riblets. Forgo adding the Rosemary Butter.

2. Tian

2½ pounds zucchini
Salt and freshly ground pepper to taste
½ cup rice, uncooked
5 Tablespoons olive oil
1 bunch green onions, finely chopped
2 large cloves garlic, minced
2 Tablespoons flour
2½ cups zucchini juice and milk, heated
⅔ cup Parmesan cheese, grated

Method

1. Trim, wash and coarsely grate zucchini. Place in a colander over a bowl, salt lightly and let drain 15 to 20 minutes. Reserve juices. While zucchini drains, cook rice in boiling salted water for exactly 5 minutes. Drain and set aside.
2. When zucchini has finished draining, squeeze remaining juices out by hand. Dry zucchini on paper towels.
3. Heat 3 Tablespoons of oil in large frying pan. Add onions and cook slowly until they are soft and transparent. Add onions and continue cooking until onions are slightly browned. Stir zucchini and garlic. Continue cooking about 5 minutes.
4. Sprinkle flour over the zucchini mixture and cook 2 minutes. Remove from heat and stir in hot liquid, blending until flour is smooth. Return to heat and bring to a simmer.
5. Stir in rice and all but 2 tablespoons of cheese.
6. Turn into a shallow, buttered baking dish. Sprinkle with cheese and dribble 2 Tablespoons olive oil over top. Bake in 425° oven about 20 to 30 minutes. Serve hot or at room temperature.

6 servings

3. Pears Stuffed with Roquefort

6 ripe pears
4 Tablespoons butter, softened
½ pound Roquefort cheese, room temperature

Method

Hollow out each pear with a corer or knife. Cream butter and cheese together. Fill pear cavities with cheese mixture and chill. When ready to serve, cut the pears into ½-inch slices.

6 servings

2

3

California Chicken

1. California Chicken

3 large chicken breasts, split, skinned and boned
Salt and lemon pepper to taste
2 tomatoes, cut in wedges
½ cup ripe black olives, sliced
½ cup onions, chopped

½ cup dry sherry
1 Tablespoon lemon juice
1 Tablespoon fresh basil, chopped*
1 Tablespoon fresh marjoram, chopped*
1 avocado, sliced
¾ cup mild Cheddar cheese, grated

Method

1. Place half of each chicken breast on a square of heavy-duty aluminum foil and sprinkle with salt and lemon pepper. Top with tomato wedges. Sprinkle with olives and onions.

2. Combine sherry, lemon juice and herbs and drizzle over chicken pieces.

3. Seal each packet and cook over medium coals until chicken is tender, about 45 minutes. Do not turn packets.

4. Open packets off the grill and add avocado and cheese. Reseal and cook just until cheese melts, about 2 to 3 minutes.

6 servings

*1 Tablespoon of fresh herb equals 1 teaspoon of dried herb.

2. Almonds on the Grill

3 Tablespoons olive oil
2 Tablespoons butter

1 cup almonds, blanched
Sea salt

Method

Heat the oil and butter in small, heavy skillet over smouldering coals. As butter foams, add almonds. Stir frequently until

almonds are a golden brown. Remove and drain on paper towels. Sprinkle with sea salt while still warm.

3. Coeur à La Crème

½ pound cream cheese, softened
½ cup cottage cheese
¼ cup confectioners' sugar

1 teaspoon vanilla
1 cup whipping cream
1 pint raspberries or strawberries
1 pint blueberries (optional)

Method

1. Beat cream cheese, cottage cheese, sugar, and vanilla together until creamy. Fold in whipped cream.

2. Line a heart-shaped coeur a la crème mold, or any other suitable basket, with cheesecloth that has been wrung out in cold water. Allow enough cloth to fold over top of mold.

3. Spoon the cheese mixture into mold, fold cloth over and refrigerate overnight on a rack over a baking sheet to catch drippings. To serve, unmold cheese on serving plate and surround with fresh berries.

6 servings

Cold Salmon Wedges

1. Cold Salmon Wedges

2 cans (¾ ounces) salmon, drained and cleaned
1 cup rice, half-cooked and drained
2 Tablespoons onion, grated
1½ teaspoons salt
½ teaspoon freshly ground pepper
2 Tablespoons parsley, chopped
2 Tablespoons fresh dill, chopped
½ cup lemon juice
2 cups milk, scalded and cooled
3 eggs, beaten
¼ cup melted butter
Garnish: dill or watercress

Method

1. Combine the salmon in a bowl with the rice, onion, salt, pepper, parsley, dill and lemon juice and mix well. Stir in milk and eggs. Turn into a 1½-quart buttered casserole and add butter.
2. Bake in a 350° oven 35 minutes, or until firm and brown on top. Chill. Cut into wedges and serve garnished with dill or watercress.

6 servings

2. Stuffed Zucchini

3 zucchini, trimmed and washed with centers scooped out
6 ears fresh corn
1 large green Bell pepper, diced
3 green onions, chopped
1 tomato, diced
6 Tablespoons olive oil
2 Tablespoons wine vinegar
¼ teaspoon Dijon-style mustard
1 teaspoon fresh thyme, chopped
Salt and freshly ground pepper to taste

Method

1. Split the zucchini lengthwise. Steam until just tender. Cool.
2. Cook the corn until just tender. Cool and cut from cobs. Mix the corn, tomato, pepper and onions in a bowl.
3. Make a vinaigrette of oil, vinegar, mustard, thyme and salt and pepper. Pour over the corn mixture and mix gently.
4. Fill the cavity of each zucchini with corn salad.

6 servings

3. Coconut-Raspberry Squares

1¾ cups all-purpose flour
½ cup sugar
¼ teaspoon salt
½ cup butter
1 egg, lightly beaten
1 cup raspberry jam

Topping

1 cup sugar
3 eggs
4 Tablespoons butter
12 ounces, moist shredded coconut

Method

1. Mix the dry ingredients and cut in butter until mixture resembles coarse corn meal. Add lightly beaten egg and mix with fork. Gather the mixture together with your hands and work it quickly and gently until it forms a dough. Press the dough evenly on the bottom of a lightly buttered 15x10x1-inch pan. Spread jam evenly over dough.
2. For topping, cream butter and sugar. Add eggs one at a time, beating well after each addition until the mixture is light and fluffy. Mix in coconut and spread over jam layer.
3. Bake in 350° oven 20 to 25 minutes, or until golden brown. Cool on a rack. Cut into squares.

48 squares

Oven Fried Chicken

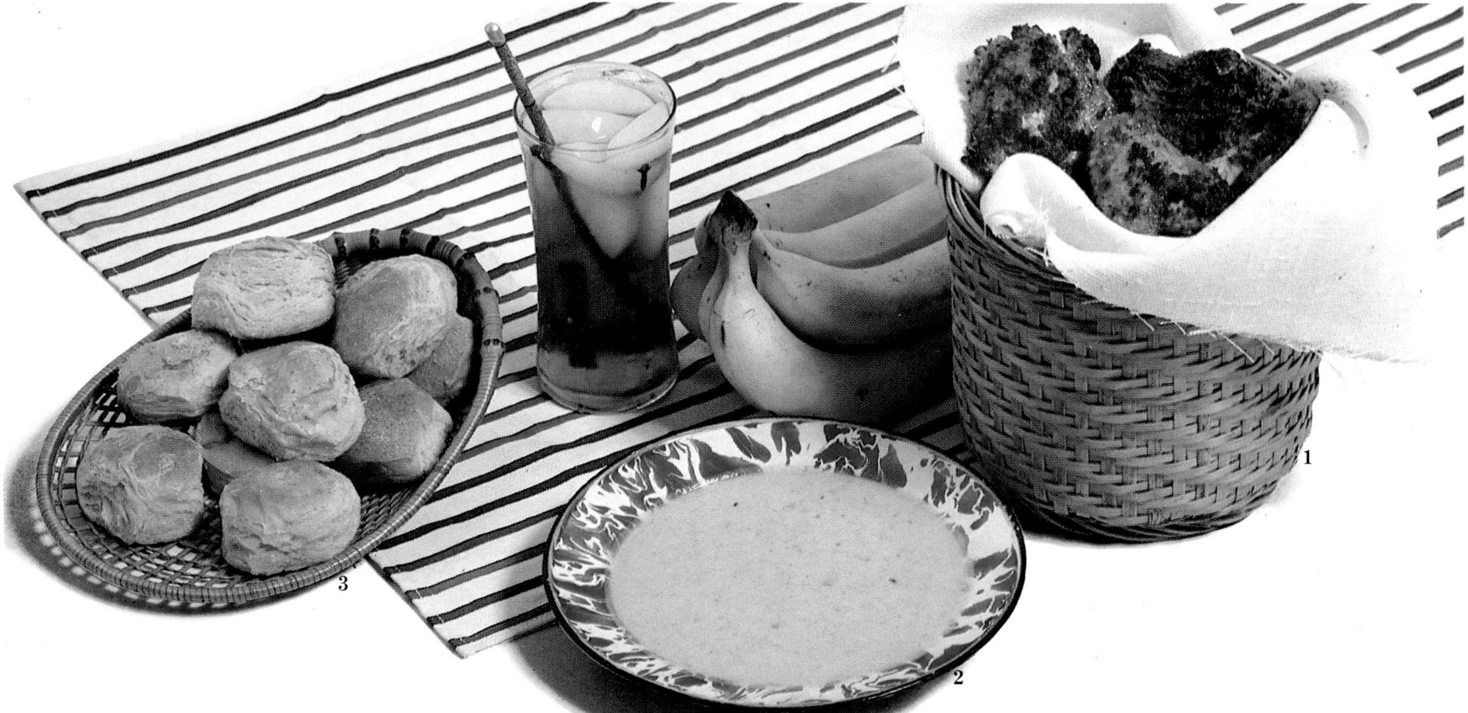

Oven Fried Chicken

1. Oven Fried Chicken

1 lemon	2 eggs, beaten
6 chicken breasts, split	Paprika
1½ cups dry stuffing mix	1 stick butter

Method

1. Squeeze lemon juice over the chicken pieces and let stand about 10 minutes. Meanwhile, pulverize stuffing mix with rolling pin to make crumbs.

2. Dip each breast in beaten egg and then into crumbs. Sprinkle with paprika.

3. Melt butter in a baking pan in a preheated 375° oven. Add the chicken, making sure pieces do not overlap. Cook 30 minutes. If chicken is not brown at the end of that time, turn oven up to 500° and cook 5 minutes longer. Serve hot or at room temperature.

6 servings

2. Cold Curried Zucchini Soup

6 Tablespoons butter	2 cups chicken broth
2 pounds zucchini, chopped	1½ cups yogurt
1 cup green onions, chopped	1½ cups light cream
1 Tablespoon curry powder	Salt and freshly ground pepper to
1 Tablespoon cumin	taste

Method

Melt butter over moderate flame. Add zucchini and green onions and cook until soft but not brown. Sprinkle with curry and cumin.

Cook an additional 2 minutes, stirring continuously. Add the chicken broth and purée in a food processor or blender. Stir in yogurt and cream. Season with salt and pepper. Chill before serving.

6 servings

3. Carolina Ham Biscuits

4 Tablespoons butter	2 teaspoons baking powder
¾ cup buttermilk	½ teaspoon baking soda
1½ cups all-purpose flour	¼ teaspoon dry mustard
	¼ pound ham, finely chopped

Method

1. Melt the butter and cool.

2. Combine all ingredients, except butter and buttermilk, in a bowl. Then stir in butter and buttermilk with a fork until dry ingredients are moist and stick together. Turn out onto lightly floured surface and knead 8 to 10 times. Roll the dough to ½-inch thickness and cut with a 2-inch biscuit cutter.

3. Bake on ungreased baking sheet in a preheated 450° oven 10 to 12 minutes, or until the biscuits rise to a golden brown color.

22 biscuits

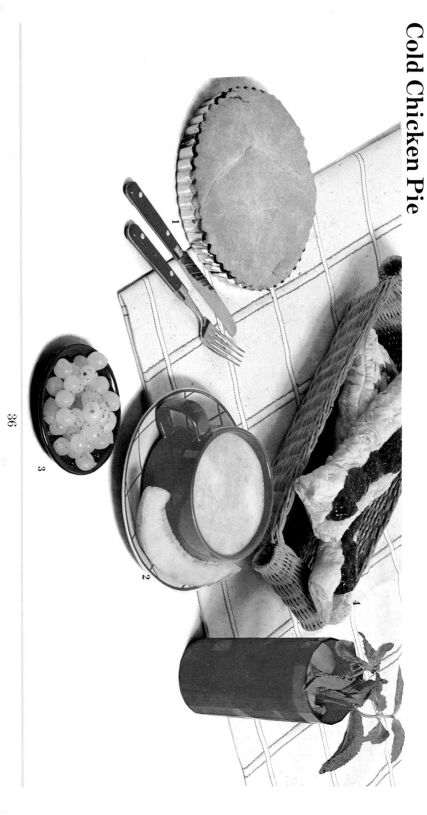

Cold Chicken Pie

1. Cold Chicken Pie

Pastry for a 2-crust, 9-inch pie
2 eggs
½ cup heavy cream
½ cup dry white wine
3 cups cooked chicken, diced

½ cup cooked peas
4 hard-cooked eggs, chopped
2 Tablespoons fresh tarragon, chopped
1 teaspoon salt
Freshly ground pepper to taste

Method

1. Line a 9-inch pie plate with half the pastry.
2. Beat the eggs, cream and wine together. Add chicken, peas, eggs, tarragon, salt and pepper and mix well.
3. Pour mixture into pie plate and cover with remaining pastry. Seal pastry edges well and make 4 gashes in top crust to let steam escape.
4. Bake in a preheated 425° oven 10 minutes. Lower heat to 350° and bake an additional 30 minutes. Cool before serving.

4 to 6 servings

2. Cantaloupe Soup

4 cups cubed cantaloupe
½ teaspoon powdered ginger
2 cups fresh orange juice

3 Tablespoons lime juice
2 cups dry white wine
Garnish : fresh mint leaves

Method

Purée the cantaloupe with ginger, orange juice and lime juice in a food processor or blender. Stir in the wine. Chill and serve garnished with fresh mint leaves.

6 servings

3. Riviera Onions

1 pound pearl onions
4 Tablespoons peanut oil
2 cloves garlic, slightly crushed

1 Tablespoon sugar
2 Tablespoons lemon juice
2 Tablespoons sherry
½ teaspoon thyme

Method

1. Peel the onions and cut a shallow cross in the stem of each.
2. Heat oil in a heavy skillet. Add onions and garlic and cook, turning occasionally, until onions are slightly browned.
3. Sprinkle the remaining ingredients over onions and cover. Continue cooking over low heat, stirring frequently, until onions are tender and sugar has turned a caramel color. Avoid burning.
4. Discard garlic and serve onions in a dish with sauce.

6 servings

4. Jam Strips

1 cup butter
1 cup sugar

6 egg yolks
2 Tablespoons lemon juice
3 cups all-purpose flour, sifted
Raspberry jam

Method

1. Cream the butter. Gradually add sugar, creaming well after each addition. Beat in the egg yolks one at a time and add lemon juice. Add flour gradually. Chill two hours.
2. Form dough into two cylinders about 1½ inches wide. Flatten slightly and indent down the length of each roll.
3. Put on a baking sheet and bake in 350° oven 12 to 15 minutes.
4. To serve, fill indentation with jam and cut 14 diagonal slices 1-inch thick.

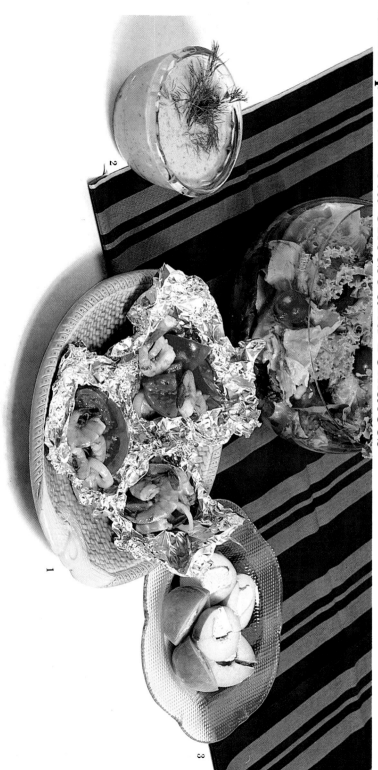

Shrimp with Feta Cheese and Tomatoes

1. Shrimp with Feta Cheese and Tomatoes

¾ cup onions, chopped
5 Tablespoons butter
3 cups canned tomatoes
1½ cups feta cheese, crumbled

1½ pounds medium shrimp, peeled
and deveined
2 Tablespoons fresh dill, finely
chopped

Method

1. Sauté the onion in butter until soft but not brown.
2. Divide tomatoes among six 12-inch squares of heavy-duty aluminum foil. Top with the shrimp, cheese and onions. Sprinkle with dill.
3. Carefully seal foil packets and place over medium coals 20 to 25 minutes, or until shrimp are opaque and sauce is blended. Do not turn packets while cooking. Serve with rice.

6 servings

2. Summer Soup

¾ cup raisins
4 cups yogurt
2 hard-cooked eggs, chopped
1 large cucumber, peeled and
chopped
2 teaspoons salt

½ teaspoon freshly ground pepper
⅓ cups green onions, chopped
1 cup of ice water
8 ice cubes
Garnish : 1 Tablespoon chopped
Chinese parsley (cilantro); 1
Tablespoon chopped fresh dill

Method

1. Soak the raisins in cold water until plump.
2. Mix the yogurt, cream, eggs, vegetables, salt and pepper in a large bowl. Drain raisins, and add with the cup of ice water and

mix well. Cover and refrigerate at least 3 hours before serving. To serve, garnish with Chinese parsley and dill.

6 servings

3. Peaches Stuffed with Strawberry Cheese

6 peaches
½ pound cream cheese, softened

½ cup strawberries, finely chopped
4 Tablespoons powdered sugar

Method

1. Halve the peaches and remove stone.
2. Blend cream cheese, strawberries, and sugar in a food processor or blender until mixture is light. Stuff peaches with mixture and chill. Cut the peaches crosswise and serve.

6 servings

39

Country Pâté

1. Country Pâté

1 pound pork fat
1 pound veal
1 pound chicken livers
2 eggs
¼ cup brandy
¼ cup whipping cream
¼ cup Madeira
1 clove garlic, finely chopped
¼ teaspoon dried thyme
¼ teaspoon dried basil
¼ teaspoon ground allspice
Salt and freshly ground pepper to taste
6 slices bacon, blanched 5 minutes in boiling water
6 bay leaves

Method

1. Put meats through food chopper or chop coarsely by hand or in food processor. Mix well with the remaining ingredients except bacon and bay leaves.

2. Place bacon in 1½-quart loaf pan. Overlap ends and press pâté mixture into pan. Cover with bacon and top with bay leaves. Bake in a preheated 325° oven, in a water bath, 2 hours. When done, a knife inserted in the center should reveal clear liquid. If bloody, cook another 30 minutes. Cool, weight* and refrigerate.

6 to 8 servings

*Place a can wrapped in aluminum foil on top of the cooled pâté. Weighting a pâté firms it up and makes it easier to slice.

2. Chilled Pimento Soup

4 Tablespoons butter
1 cup onion, chopped
4 Tablespoons flour
8 ounces canned pimentos
2 cups whipping cream
Salt and freshly ground pepper to taste
Garnish : fresh chives or parsley

Method

1. Over medium heat, sauté the onion in melted butter until soft but not brown. Stir in flour and continue cooking for one minute. Avoid burning the flour.

2. Add the chicken broth and cook, stirring constantly until thickened. Remove from heat and stir in pimentos. Purée in food processor or blender.

3. Add cream and season to taste. Chill. Serve garnished with fresh chopped chives or parsley.

6 to 8 servings

Watercress Sandwiches

2 bunches watercress
1 loaf day-old bread, uncut
1 stick soft butter

Method

1. Rinse and drain watercress. Pat dry and trim leaves from stems.

2. Slice off heel of the bread. Spread the white portion of the bread end thinly with butter. Cut off a thin slice. Repeat until all bread is cut. Trim crusts and divide slices in half.

3. Place several watercress leaves on bread slices and top with another slice or leave open faced. These sandwiches can be prepared several hours ahead of time but do not refrigerate. Store on a tray covered with a damp towel until ready to serve.

Grilled Eggplant Sandwiches

Grilled Eggplant Sandwiches

1 large eggplant
Salt to taste
½ pound prosciutto, thinly sliced
½ pound Mozzarella cheese, sliced
2 eggs, lightly beaten

1 cup dry bread crumbs, finely ground
¼ cup fresh basil, finely chopped
¼ cup Parmesan cheese, grated
4 Tablespoons olive oil

Method

1. Wash and trim the eggplant. Cut into 1-inch slices. Salt the slices and weigh them down with a plate 1 hour. Rinse well and dry.

2. Top with proscuitto and cheese. Sprinkle with bread crumbs, basil and Parmesan. Dribble oil on top. Place on a hinged grill and set over medium hot coals about 30 minutes, turning once. Serve hot or at room temperature.

4 to 6 servings

2. Tortellini Salad

2 packages (15 ounces) frozen tortellini (fresh if you can find it)
6 green onions, chopped
3 canned pimentos, julienned
½ pound baked ham, cut into ¼-inch slices and julienned
2 Tablespoons pine nuts

Dill Dressing

2 Tablespoons fresh dill, chopped
1 egg yolk
1 teaspoon Dijon-style mustard
1 Tablespoon lemon juice
1 Tablespoon white wine vinegar
2 Tablespoons heavy cream
1½ cups olive oil
Salt and freshly ground pepper to taste

Method

1. Cook tortellini and cool. Mix with onions, pimentos, ham and pine nuts and toss with dressing.

2. For dressing, mix all ingredients except olive oil in blender. Slowly add oil while still blending. Refrigerate until ready to use.

6 to 8 servings

3. Oatmeal Cookies

2 eggs
1 cup butter, melted
2 Tablespoons maple syrup
1 teaspoon baking soda

1 teaspoon cinnamon
2 cups rolled oats
1 cup raisins
3 cups flour
¼ cup hot water

Method

Beat eggs. Mix in remaining ingredients. Drop on buttered baking sheet and flatten out. Bake in 325° oven about 15 minutes.

4 dozen

Roquefort Steak

1. Roquefort Steak

Steak for grilling
¼ pound Roquefort cheese
4 Tablespoons butter
½ teaspoon Worchestershire sauce
2 Tablespoons chives, chopped

Method

1. Grill steak to desired doneness.
2. For Roquefort Butter, cream butter and cheese together.
Blend in remaining ingredients and chill. Serve steaks spread
with prepared butter.

2. Salt-roasted Potatoes

10 cups coarse (Kosher) salt
8 baking potatoes
Lard

Method

Add enough water to salt to form a thick paste. Rub potatoes
with lard and pat with paste. After coating, set potatoes directly
in embers and bake about 1 hour. Break off salt coating when
served.

8 servings

3. Tomatoes with Fresh Basil

6 large vine-ripened tomatoes,
thinly sliced
9 Tablespoons pure olive oil
3 Tablespoons wine vinegar
1 red onion sliced
8 Tablespoons fresh basil, coarsely
chopped (parsley, tarragon,
marjoram)
Salt and freshly ground pepper to
taste

Method

Arrange tomatoes in a salad bowl. Sprinkle each layer with
remaining ingredients.

6 to 8 servings

Tandoori Chicken

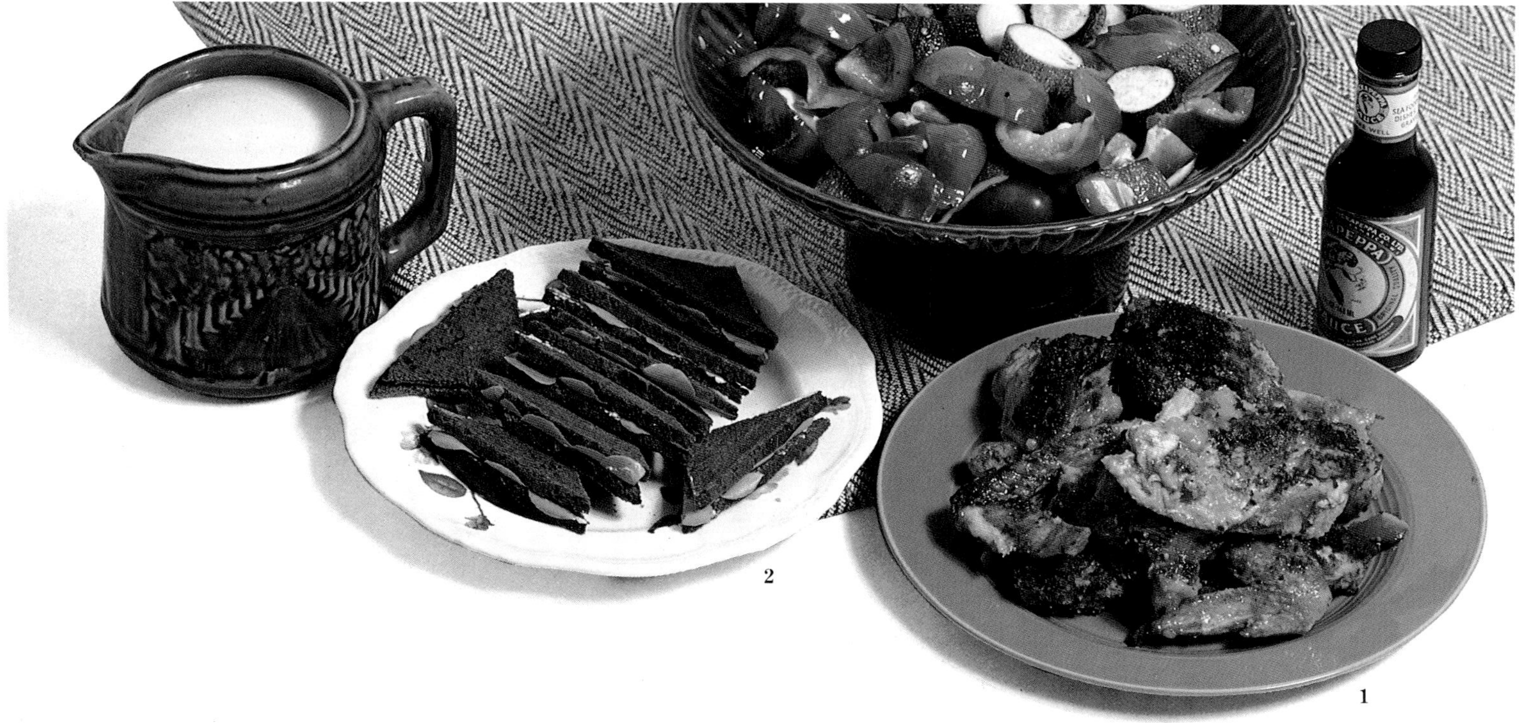